# What Is
# Veterans Day?

By Margot Parker

*Illustrated by Matt Bates*

CHILDRENS PRESS®

CHICAGO

Library of Congress Cataloging-in-Publication Data

Parker, Margot.
    What is Veterans Day.

    Summary: Ben explains to Amy why we celebrate
Veterans Day each year.
    1.  Veterans Day—Juvenile literature.  [1.  Veterans
Day]  I.  Title.
D671.P36   1986        394.2'684        86-11732
ISBN 0-516-03782-X

"Hi, Ben," said Amy.
"May I help you?"

"Sure, Amy," said Ben.

4

"Do you want to join my parade?"

5

"Oh, yes!" cried Amy. "But why are we having a parade?"

"Amy, don't you know?"
exclaimed Ben. "Tomorrow
is Veterans Day."

"What is Veterans Day, Ben?"

"Well," said Ben, "We celebrate Veterans Day on November 11 of each year."

"Why?"

"Because it reminds us

to say thanks to all
the brave men and women

who loved
our country
enough to
serve in the
Armed Forces."

CANADA

AMERICA

MEXICO

"Armed Forces?
What's that?" Amy asked.

"It's the army...

navy...

marines...

air force, and

coast guard."

"Why did the United States
have men and women serve in
the Armed Forces?" Amy asked.

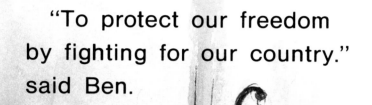

"To protect our freedom
by fighting for our country."
said Ben.

6
8
2
3

"Freedom means being
able to go to school,

21

church, and

22

other places we like.

"Freedom means being able
to live where we want...

25

to have the jobs that we want...

29

and to make money," said Ben.

"On Veterans Day we
celebrate by having parades...

by placing flowers on military
graves, and by giving speeches,"
explained Ben.

"In the United States special services
are celebrated in Arlington, Virginia
at the tomb of the Unknown Soldier,"
said Ben.

TOMB OF THE
UNKNOWN SOLDIER

"What's the Tomb of the
Unknown Soldier, Ben?"
asked Amy.

"It's a place where a soldier who died for our country is buried," said Ben.

"Ben, do other countries have a special place to bury their soldiers?" asked Amy.

"Sure, Amy. In France the
unknown soldier is buried
at the Arc de Triomphe in Paris.

"Great Britain buried
its unknown soldier
in Westminster Abbey.

"Italy's unknown soldier is buried in front of the monument of Victor Emmanuel in Rome," said Ben.

"Ben, do other countries
celebrate Veterans Day, too?"
asked Amy.

"Yes, France and Great Britain celebrate on November 11 and call it Armistice Day. Canada calls November 11 Remembrance Day," explained Ben.

"In the United States President
Woodrow Wilson called November 11,
Armistice Day, a day to honor
our veterans who served in
World War I."

"Ben, if there was a World War I—
was there a World War II?"
asked Amy.

"Yes, Amy, a World War II, a Korean War, and a Vietnam War. In 1954 Congress changed the name from Armistice Day to Veterans Day," said Ben. "In order to honor *all* the people who fought for the United States."

"Thanks, Ben, now I know why
we honor the veterans from
each war on November 11,"
said Amy.

"Come on, Ben, we've had enough
wars. Let's get some kids to
join our Veterans Day parade!"
cried Amy.

"Right on!" said Ben.

## THE AUTHOR

**Margot Parker** has been a kindergarten teacher with Sacramento City Schools for more than twenty years. She is a graduate of California State University at Sacramento, is married, and has two grown children. Her search for illustrated books that explain why people celebrate special days prompted her to write *What Is Columbus Day?* for young children. *What Is Veterans Day?* is the second book in the *What Is* series.

## THE ILLUSTRATOR

**Matt Bates** has studied art at Cosumnes River College in Sacramento and the California Institute of the Arts in Valencia. He also has studied under Louis Gadaul and with several Walt Disney animators, including Hal Ambro, T. Hee, and Bob McCrea. He is currently working as a staff artist with Marvel Productions in Van Nuys, California.